This book belongs to
Mr. Glasgow

TIME FOR KIDS®

 BEGINNING 1 READER *Science Scoops*

Bees!

By the Editors of TIME FOR KIDS
WITH ELIZABETH WINCHESTER

 HarperCollins*Publishers*

About the Author: An editor at TIME FOR KIDS®, Elizabeth Winchester has written about everything from planets and politics to bullies and dog shows. She lives with her husband, Chris, and dog, Reggie, in New York City.

To Teresa Pickman and Chris Winchester, for helping me to keep my cool when the bees buzz.

Special thanks to bee expert Charles Michener, Ph.D., for his time, insight, and suggestions.
—E.W.

Library of Congress Cataloging-in-Publication Data is available.
ISBN 0-06-057642-1 (pbk.) — ISBN 0-06-057643-X (trade)

1 2 3 4 5 6 7 8 9 10
First Edition

Photography and Illustration Credits:
Cover: Michael Durham; cover insert: Scott Camazine; cover flap: Wolfgang Schmidt—Peter Arnold; title page: H. Zettl—Zefa/Masterfile; pg. 3: Mitsuhiko Imamori—Minden; pp. 4–5: James Robinson—Animals Animals; pp. 6–7: SuperStock; pp. 8–9: SuperStock; pp. 10–11: John T. Fowler—Alamy; pp. 12–13: Kim Taylor—Bruce Coleman; pp. 14–15: Dennis McDonald—Alamy; pp. 16–17: Terje Rakke—Getty Images; pg. 17 (inset): John Courtney; pp. 18–19: Steve Hopkin—Getty Images; pp. 20–21: E. S. Ross—Visuals Unlimited; pp. 22–23: Scott Camazine; pg. 23 (inset): Barbara Spurll; pp. 24–25: Ken Lucas—Visuals Unlimited; pp. 26–27: Alan Ward—Livingston County Daily Press & Argus/AP; pp. 28–29: Lynda Richardson—Corbis; pp. 30–31: Bach—Zefa/Masterfile; pg. 32 (antennae): Mitsuhiko Imamori—Minden; pg. 32 (colonies): Ken Lucas—Visuals Unlimited; pg. 32 (hives): Alan Ward—Livingston County Daily Press & Argus/AP; pg. 32 (honeycomb): Ken Lucas—Visuals Unlimited; pg. 32 (nectar): SuperStock; pg. 32 (pollen): SuperStock.

Acknowledgments:
For TIME FOR KIDS: Editorial Director: Keith Garton; Editor: Nelida Gonzalez Cutler; Art Director: Rachel Smith; Photography Editor: Jill Tatara

HarperCollins books may be purchased for educational, business, or sales promotional use. For information, please write: Special Markets Department, HarperCollins Publishers Inc., 10 East 53rd Street, New York, NY 10022.

 Check us out at **www.timeforkids.com**

What's that buzzing?
It sounds like a bee!

Bees are insects.
They have six legs
and four wings.
When a bee flies, its wings
make a buzzing sound.

Bees use their antennas to smell.
They use their front legs
and long tongue to taste.
Bees sip a juice called nectar
from flowers.

Bees also eat pollen from flowers.
They carry pollen to other flowers.
This helps flowers make seeds!

There are many kinds of bees.
Bees can be black, yellow, or red.
They can even be blue or bright green!

Leafcutter bees are big bees.
They can be up to
one and one-half inches long.
But some bees are very small.
You can hardly see them!

Bees live almost everywhere.
They do not live at the
North and South Poles.
Bees build homes called nests.

Honeybees live in groups called colonies.
Beekeepers build homes for honeybees.
These homes are called hives.

That Is Amazing!

As many as 70,000 bees can live in one hive.
That is about as many people as go to
the Superbowl!

Each bee in a hive has an important job!
There is one queen bee in each hive.
She is the biggest bee in the hive.

Male honeybees mate with the queen.
Then she lays eggs.
In less than a month,
an adult bee comes out.

Other female honeybees are workers.
Worker bees clean and protect the hive.
They take care of the young.
They bring back food for others.

That Is Amazing!

Only female bees have a stinger.
Worker honeybees sting only once,
and then die.

Honeybees use nectar to make honey.
Workers put nectar into honeycomb cells.
The cells are tiny rooms made of wax.

The nectar turns into honey!
Bees eat some of the honey.
Beekeepers collect the rest from the hive.

We eat honey that we get from honeybees.
We also get beeswax.
It is used to make crayons and candles.

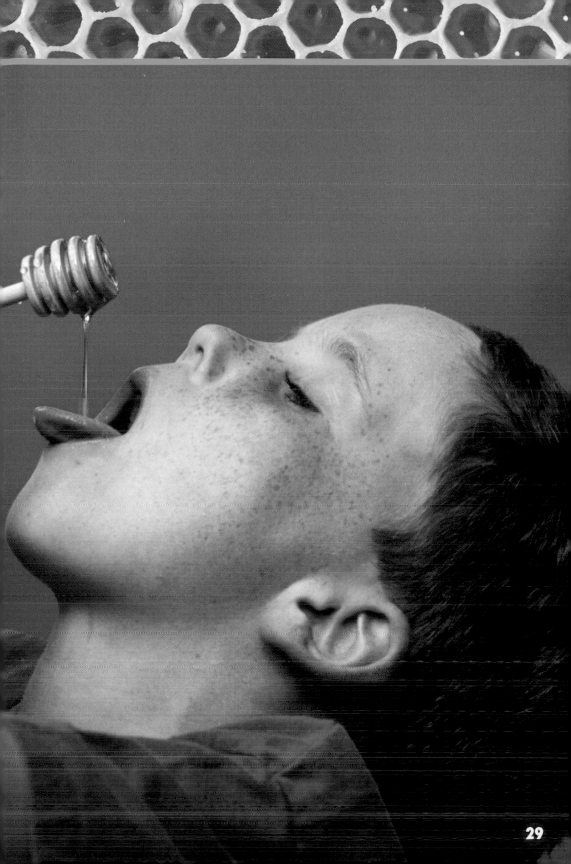

Bees help make the world more beautiful. Hooray for bees!

WORDS to Know

Antennas: feelers that stick out from an insect's head

Honeycomb: wax rooms where honeybees store honey

Colonies: groups of bees that live and work together

Nectar: sweet liquid from flowers

Hives: homes that beekeepers build for honeybees

Pollen: tiny, powdery grains that flowers make